Table of Content

Introduction

An estimation of 12.5 million Africans were purloined from the continent of Africa and of that 12.5 million, approximately, 388,000 were brought to what would eventually become the United States of America. These Africans were not all from one territory in Africa, nor were they of the same ethnic group. From historical documents and DNA results it has been determined that these Africans came from 20 countries in west Africa, between Senegal and Angola, which are comprised of nearly 167 ethnic groups. They spoke different languages and liked different things. These Africans were not only distinct in their origin, languages, and cultures but in their status as well. Their status, in their homelands, ranged from royalty, to soldiers, to merchants, to artisans;

likewise, some were educated and proficient in medicine and agriculture. Once in the new world these Africans had thorny continuations; yet, in some instances the experiences were marginally diverse. Some Africans managed to escape bondage. Some were able to purchase their freedom. There are reports of some who were released by those who owned them; needless to say, not all Africans were positioned to procure their freedom. While the majority of Africans lived on restricted rural plantations there were those who lived in cities, and their being was just as challenging and just as brutal. Then there were those few Africans who managed to not only gain their freedom, but they were able to expand their status by purchasing African slaves.

Once slavery ended some African families managed to secure farmland, opened stores to sale their products, and offer other services; thus, establishing themselves as profitable businesspeople. Newly freed Africans were not all farmers, some fortunate Africans were able to live well by capitalizing on talents they acquired as bondsmen; talents such as laundry, tailoring, carpentry, shoe making, black smiths, barbering, cooking, brick masons, and even lumber mill owners. Then there were those who founded cities and still others who were able to attain white collar positions, which afforded those Africans, to prosper. These white-collar abilities were in lawyering, teaching, pastoring, politics, and journalism.

Today, African Americans are a familiar motley of Americans who descended from those enslaved Africans, who were brought from the coast of West Africa. The point of this brief analysis, regarding the morphation of Africans into African Americans, is not to ebb their arduous journey; instead, it is to emphasize the matter that African Americans have never been a myopic people.

When Africans were still in their homeland, before they arrived in the new world, they had distinct voices and their voices amplified once they became free. Nine Voices of African Americans is not a complete representation of African American life and culture. There are way more voices of African Americans than nine and African Americans have assorted means of attaining income; and, some African Americans have acquired great wealth while many have not. African Americans have different political agendas, and their forms of entertainment, loving, recreation, and relaxation are sundry. *9 Voices of African Americans* is an attempt to legitimize those unique voices in hopes that African Americans continue to broaden their minds, grow their dreams, and continue to explore every field of endeavor.

The gumption to survive,
hold your head up high
the will to stay alive;
convert handicaps into a lie.
Employ adversity to thrive,
keep going never ask why,
Let others ponder where comes your drive.

The Hughes Mantra

1ˢᵗ Voice

My New Day is the first voice, it is an exhilarating but unpredictable roller coaster ride that many identify as Black love. This first voice is about what Black love has been, what it is, and what it can become. Only 36% of African American couples raise their children in the same house.[1] Black men and women possess tender spirits and fiery radical hearts but it appears they lack the human interfacing skills needed to maintain the sensitivity and compassion that are required to forge a lasting family bond.

When Africans were brought to America they were stripped of their ethnicity and culture. Today, DNA technology can link African Americans back to their

---

[1] https://ifstudies.org/blog/the-majority-of-us-children-still-live-in-two-parent-families

heritage, and with this knowledge, they can use the symbols and ancient landmarks of their past to build a better today and an even more promising tomorrow.

My New Day

The time was 10:00 p.m. you had just crawled into your bed, wearing those big blue and yellow rollers in your hair. You were also wearing a knee-length Sponge Bob Square pants night shirt, as you waited for the sandman to arrive.

The time became 10:13 p.m. I was wearing my green and silk undershirt along with my gray and red boxer shorts. I had dropped hard onto my bed like a thought that plunges deep into one's mind.

The time then changed to 10:15 p.m. and sleep was on the both of us, at the exact same time.

We were dreaming; and (by fate's decree) we met in each other's dream on a deserted tropical island. We were inhaling a pure, sweet, and seductive oxygen, like non other our nostrils had ever encountered. The ground looked like dirt, but it felt like one of those genuine hand crafted ancient Egyptian rugs, that makes one believe that he or she is walking on a cloud. We could not see them, but we could hear and understand tropical monkeys and birds as they spoke of love and brotherhood, as no man had ever done.

And then for the first time, I was seriously focused on you. You were seriously focused on me, and we both notice that neither one of us were wearing a stitch of clothing. But we did not travel in that direction because that was not what this dream

was about. We spoke. We introduced ourselves.
And started talking and walking and walking for at
least 400 miles. What was so amazing was that our
conversation was so stimulating and interesting that
we never paused in speech or thought about the
time, place, distance, or fatigue. It was not until we
were faced with a freshwater stream, that we
admitted that our throats were getting dry. So, we
stooped down, cupped our hands, scooped, and
drank of that soft untainted water that was cool,
refreshing and thirst quenching. After we drank of
that remarkable liquid, we turned and saw a large
bolder shaped like a Sears Roebuck love seat; we
walked over to it just to find out that it is smooth,
delicate, and as comfortable as the thrown Queen
Nefertari and her husband Ahmose sat upon in
Egypt. We sat and began to talk some more.

As we talked, I made a joke. No, I made a few jokes; and you were just laughing and laughing. Then for the first time (while you were just laughing) I noticed the fullness and firmness of your big beautiful Black breasts. I noticed that your wholesome Black smooth areolas serves as a base from your deliciously delicate swelling nipples. By now you had stopped laughing and noticed that my erectile tissue was gorged with blood. Because of my instrument's potential and stability, you had become romantically inclined towards me. So, I kissed you. You kissed me back. While we were kissing, I showed no dignity whatsoever, foolhardily started caressing that lower part that you loved to have caressed. Because I am somewhat reckless in my actions, you very gently, politely and in a lady-like manner moved my hand to the side. We stopped kissing and continued to talk for another hour or so.

When all of a sudden, the ebony that was in your eyes grabbed a hold to the dark drown that was in mine. For a moment I thought the earth stood still. No, I am positive that the Earth stood still. I am positive. Do you remember that warm, soft, and consistent breeze that had earlier oiled our bodies? Well, it had all of a sudden fallen still on my face. At that moment, I do not remember leaning towards you and I do not remember you leaning towards me either yet somehow, we managed to lock into another kiss. I mean we kissed and kissed for an awfully long time. Our kiss was so strong and forceful that after a while I could hear and smell each trickle of your joyous but innocent juice that slid down your thighs, and it made the peach fuzz on my back erect. This time I decided to move very cautiously, very carefully and very slowly. So, very gently, I put my hand back on that spot that you moved it from about an hour earlier. Only, this time you let it remain. In fact, you were vigorously and madly caressing that part of me that just loved to be caressed. By now I felt that old wild, evil dirty hump developing in my back. That was when I knew the timing and feeling was coming close. I knew they were close because I could see them just as clearly as I could see a need for ecstasy. Then all of a sudden and still even at this moment I cannot tell you if it was destiny or a fool's whim. You can call it what you want. The fact of the matter is that I elected to stop. The reason I chose to stop was that I wanted to intellectualize the situation.

I pulled away from your strong, firm, but passionate grip. Another short story within itself would be how I managed to pry my leg from under yours. As I accomplished these feats, you seemed shocked and surprised. But, at the same time, you seemed to be proud and pleased to witness my refrain from a base and lascivious desire to have you before I would accept or give a sincere commitment. Before you could say a word, your alarm clock beckoned you to awaken and in your beautiful little ebony eyes, I could see you saying that time has not run out on us because this is only the beginning of a new day; yet, your lips very gently, politely, and still in a lady like manner, apologized to me. Before you left you took time to whisper into my ear, "If one has the power, will, and discipline to control ones' dream, then that one has the power, will, and discipline to control the world." Then you left me alone to think. And it was at that moment that I realized that I do love you.

I Love You!

I love you, not because of any sexual feelings or any of your physical features. Although I must admit that your beauty is more mysterious than the pyramids, more exotic than the Congo and you are more sensuous than Queen Moremi. Even the sun and the moon have told me that your mortal beauty was more exquisite than any other creature they have ever laid rays upon. Nevertheless, I was not in love with your outer appearance. What I loved about you was your attitude, your behavior, your disposition, your thoughts, your likes, and your dislikes. I remember back at the 99 ½ Mile mark that I asked if you were prepared to meet the unexpected. Then you, with the wisdom of Yaa Asantewaa, the sophistication of Hatshepsut, and the astuteness of Phyllis Wheatley, asked me, " How does one prepare oneself for the unexpected, when the unexpected never comes when one expects it?" It is that brilliance and quick wit that has blown my nose, ears, eyes, and heart wide open all out of proportion.

It was then I realized that you are a very stimulating conversationalist; it was also then that I realized that from the beginning of my existence I have been yearning for your intellectual companionship. I guess that is why I find it hard to believe that for the last four hundred years, I have been deliberately and systematically brainwashed to believe that you are nothing more than a godless, cheap, Black whore who is supposed to be nothing more to me than a breeding partner. I said this is hard to believe because today I know for a fact that you, the Black woman is God's greatest gift, not only to the world and to the universe but to me also. It was behind that very sacred thought that my alarm clock goes off. Consequently, I was then faced with the fact that I was dreaming.

I know I was dreaming because in reality the Black man and woman do not live in harmony. We do not respect, love, or honor one another as we should. Nor do we build, expect, or accept an honest and intimate relationship from each other. But wait a minute!! I am a Black man. And if I can dream it, then I can live it "for life is but a dream."

So now, I know in my heart that I can respect, adore, and love my black woman the way I am designed to.

Time has not run out on me yet; and in reality, this is only the beginning of "My New Day".

2nd Voice

This second voice pertains to the international loathing of Black skin and "African" features. The intention of this second voice is to accentuate the exquisite nature of Blackness. In ancient Egypt and Greece, Black had positive connotations. Black was the first color humans used in art and it was the color that symbolized fertility. This second voice is a reminder that Black is beautiful, intelligent, sensuous, warm, sexy, and Black is an aphrodisiac.

Black Beauty

His first encounter with her was from afar. It was her strong, distinctive, and melodic voice he heard gliding from across the room. In her voice he detected a profound spiritual understanding as well as an extremely high intellectual essence. Without turning his head toward, the voice, he allowed his ears to lead him in the direction toward the voice of God. When he finally laid eyes on this Goddess, that emitted the voice of heaven, he knew he had finally witnessed pure love.

Her skin was three shades exceeding black but not a dull black; instead, she boasted a soft black. Her skin juxtaposed her voice; although her voice was strong her skin was soft and supple. In her skin he saw sexiness, finesse, and loveliness.

As he walked closer, he watched her talking to those gathered grasping the sweet verses that sprung from her tongue, like tappers catching palm wine. The first thing he noticed about her was how the incandescent light complimented her smooth forehead. The gleam on her forehead performed as a spotlight for her warm and piercing eyes which gave her the appearance of a wise soul. The rest of her face was smooth and slim (not one blemish). As she spoke, he fell in love with her smile. Her smile was witty and enticing with teeth so white and straight that any dentist would marvel over the craftsmanship.

3rd Voice

This third voice is about family. Not knowing and understanding is the connotation for bliss. Once truth is revealed does the revelation altar genuine affection? No. Mature love is stronger than fanciful fondness. If the love is real, then nothing should change. Real love is knowing the truth about something and still maintaining a high level of respect and adoration for it.

He Is Not My Type

All my life I heard my mother say, "Your dad is a bum." When it came to my dad I never listened to my mom. What she said about boys panned out, as well as things regarding health and my friends; but when it came to my dad, I turned a death ear. I ignored my mom's view of my dad mainly because a few of my friends did not know their dad and the others who knew of their dad rarely saw him. Of course, I had some friends who lived with their dad, but I did not compare my experience with theirs. My dad was always in my life. I never understood why my dad did not live with my mom and me. He never missed any of my birthdays. I got plenty of gifts for Christmas. He even gave me gifts for Valentines. Whether it was a school function or sporting event, if I was in it, my dad was there. My favorite gift, from my dad, was a pair of bright pink panties with a dark purple bow on front. On the day I received my pink panties I still remember being angry with my mom; as I fingered the purple bow on my panties, she spewed the customary: "He's a bum." Before she could finish her favorite phrase, I made a very spirited demand. I remembered that she was my mom but this time she made me angry. How dare she spoil my moment with my bright pink panties and dark purple bow? "Why do you hate him?" She did not look at me and by the tone of her response I knew I would not be reprimanded for my vociferation. She looked into space and said: "He's not your type." At that age I had no idea what she meant and from the obscure and faraway look on her face it was apparent she was not talking to me.

From then on, I consciously and openly praised my dad; yet, my mom never made another derogating statement about my dad, at least not in my presence. When I got older, got my first job, and my first paycheck, I borrowed my mom's car to take my dad shopping. When I arrived at his place to pick him up, I told him: "I'm taking you shopping, what you want?" He said: "Good, I need some new drawers."

 I took my dad to an upscale department store with hopes that I could find some underwear that he would keep as fondly as I did those bright pink panties with the dark purple bow that he had given me. When we arrived in the store, I walked ahead of my dad and found a pleasing and dignified 3 pack of underwear for $17. Immediately my dad looked around and I was befuddled when he asked, "Where the $3 drawers?" I said, "Dad, I'm buying these for you." He left me standing there, waved over a store employee, and asked, "Where yo $3 drawers?" Before the person could answer I grabbed my dad by the arm and said, "Dad, I'm buying these let's go." He protested, "Oh hell no, let's go to the thrift store. That's where I get all my drawers." Before I knew it, I snapped, "Dad, that's disgusting. I don't believe you buy used underwear!" I believe if he had looked in my face he would have saw the abhorrence I displayed and maybe then he would not have continued to protest; instead, he looked in the direction of the packs of $17 and $36 underwear and said, "Baby Girl, they got some good stuff there, remember those pink panties with the purple bow? I got those from the thrift store." At that very moment I was done with my dad. I grabbed that pack of $17 underwear, I told my dad, "Let's go". I paid for the underwear. Drove him to his place. I went home. Gave my mom her car keys. I went to my room and cried. Until this day I have been too embarrassed to tell anybody about that ordeal. Not even my mom knows how irritated and furious I was with my dad. I cried so much I was exhausted; but, before I fell asleep, I reflected on my dad I settled on the fact that I still loved him but he is not my type.

4th Voice

The fourth and fifth voices were inspired by my late sister-in-law, Lydia Phillips. She was the first African American, that I knew, who had embraced Country Music. For a time, she was learning how to play country music chords on an acoustic guitar. She was learning to ride horses. And, she even procured front row tickets to see Charley Pride.

In popular music a song can be described as a short poem set to music; in contrast, a Country song is usually arranged as a melodic ballad, neatly woven into a simple story. This fourth voice is to be envisioned as a complicated, upbeat, fast tempo, 1-4-5 with an acoustic and electric guitar lead, being chased by drums, fiddle, piano, harmonica, and bass guitar.

Last Call For Alcohol

<u>1st Verse</u>

It's "Lady's Night"

I'm getting in free

I'm going straight to the bar

And drink myself to sleep.

Girls don't get offended

If I'm not paying attention.

I'm not saying you're boring

I just want to see

The Bartender's hand pouring.

<u>Chorus</u>

The DJ said, "Last call for alcohol"

Which was something I most feared

I asked, "Oh, so now I gotta go home?"

He said "No, but you gotta get the hell out of here!"

2nd Verse

For me this has been a long week

I just found out that neither

My job nor my man wants to commit.

I'm drinking Gin, Vodka, Whiskey

All the hard stuff,

I don't want no beer

Because beer my friend

Just ain't strong enough.

I'm having a good time,

The drinks are wonderful

I'm convinced this place is my fate,

The whole club cheered

When the nice young DJ

Let me announce my age & weight.

Chorus

The DJ said, "Last call for alcohol"

Which was something I most feared

I asked, "Oh, so now I gotta go home?"

He said "No, but you gotta get the hell out of here!"

3rd Verse

The night has gotten long

But the liquor is still strong.

This real cute guy

Wants to know my name,

I told him "Sure but first honey

You got to buy me a hurricane."

Now he and I are on the dance floor

I even had the nerve to do a twirl,

My head started spinning

My stomach was upset

So, I had to go call "Earl".

Instead of the women's stall

I used the closest wall

To relieve myself of all my good fun;

Embarrassed? Hell no, but I'm upset

For throwing up all my good Rum.

<u>Chorus</u>

The DJ said, "Last call for alcohol"

Which was something I most feared

I asked, "Oh, so now I gotta go home?"

He said "No, but you gotta get the hell out of here!"

5th Voice

This fifth voice is another Lydia enthused country music ditty. Unlike the fourth voice, this voice is to be envisioned as a somber tempo with melancholy lyrics. Also imagine the acoustic guitar establishing a straightforward rhythm, while the organ and pedal-steel guitar creates the groove and melody. Once the time signature forms a feel, visualize the drums, mandolin, fiddle, keyboard, synthesizer, bass, and electric guitars cementing the accompaniment.

How Old Was Cinderella?

1st Verse

She'd known sadness and abuse even as a little girl,

Love and happiness were not a part of her world.

Her prince came and gave her a wonderful life,

He took her to his kingdom and made her his wife.

Chorus

How old was Cinderella?

How long should I wait for my fella?

I want him to come

While I'm still vibrant and young.

I want to be like Cinderella,

I want to be happy as well;

I want to be like Cinderella,

Don't tell me it's just a fairytale.

2nd Verse

Fairy godmother I have a broken heart for you to mend,

And I have a need for a kind and gentle friend.

Tender kisses, warm soul, strong, and passionate hand,

I want him to be a thoughtful and understanding man.

Chorus

How old was Cinderella?

How long should I wait for my fella?

I want him to come

While I'm still vibrant and young.

I want to be like Cinderella,

I want to be happy as well;

I want to be like Cinderella,

And don't tell me it's just a fairytale.

3rd Verse

While I still have strength, I want to ride his horse

I need to do it soon before I develop remorse.

I want to meet him now while I'm still full of laughter,

Like Cinderella, I want to live happily ever after.

Chorus

How old was Cinderella?

How long should I wait for my fella?

I want him to come

While I'm still vibrant and young.

I want to be like Cinderella,

I want to be happy as well;

I want to be like Cinderella,

Don't tell me it's just a fairytale.

6th Voice

This 6th voice is an affirmation to the spiritual conflict of African Americans. When Africans were brought to the new world they had a traditional West African cultural belief system. Upon their arrival into the new world, Africans had to endure a brutal seasoning process which included them being methodically purged of their names, languages, and cultures; surprisingly, Africans never abandoned their belief in god; not during their darkest days, not when they had to trod stony roads, and not even as they suffered the bitter chastening rod. As their identification terms transmuted from Colored, to Negro, to African American, they were steadfast in their worship of a supreme being whom they perceived as owner of creation, the principal object of faith, and the source of all virtue and moral obligations.

African Americans originated from different ethnic groups in West Africa and it was a traditional West African cultural belief that the progenitor, of the universe, was devoid of color or gender; ironically, Africans were forced to convert into a belief system where the divine creator, of all life, is a white man.

What Color Is God

White men brought me to these shores as chattel flesh,

I've been beat, sold, castrated, and lynched.

I've witnessed my mother raped;

My father burned at the stake,

And my woman used as a nigger bed wench.

What did I do to deserve all this?

I hue the wood, draw the water,

And say my prayers every night;

But I've come to the conclusion that my fate is sealed,

Because the god I worship is white.

I was born a Baptist and as far as I can conceive,

My Christianity has been the cause of my wretchedness,

So, I looked to the east thinking Allah would be best;

But I found that Tippu Tib and his Muslim brothers

Treated my east African cousins

Worst then the Christians treated me out west.

Marcus Messiah Garvey and the Black Panther Party

Tried so hard to deliver me,

But when the devil became impatient

He flexed his muscle

And maneuvered them into a tight jam;

When my heroes where discredited & disrupted

I accepted that fact,

That if you're black,

God does not give a damn.

Imagine if you will

You relaxing in your home;

When you detect a phone ringing

But you don't have a phone.

So, you turn your house inside out

Trying to find that bell;

Well that's my situation

Institutionalized racism is so elusive

Until it has turned my life into a living hell.

So, I turned to drugs and alcohol to bliss my mind

Thinking bliss would bring my sanity back;

And I was almost there until some fool told me:

"God is not white but black".

Now I'm more confused than hell

And I'm hurting as well.

I liked it better when I perceived god as white;

At least I could explain my situation

I knew why I had a bad day,

Now I don't know my left from my right.

Why would a Black God let them shake me raggedy,

Destroy my children,

And butcher me like a hog?

I'm only hired for manual labor,

I live in subsidized housing,

And this makes me feel lower than a dog.

But one day I went to the free clinic doctor

And he introduced me to my heart;

I found that its rhythmic contractions

Have been keeping me alive from the start.

After further studying,

I found that my brain is just as powerful as a computer

And my soul is identical to the sun;

Love is not something I play as a sport,

Yet being in love is a ton of fun.

When you mix the luster of the moon

With July's warmth,

You get a color that is so unique;

I'm through deifying these earthly gods of color,

For my true salvation is here, within me.

7th Voice

During the Paleolithic Age (Old Stone Age) 200,000 BC-10,000 BC, humans established themselves in close knit clans that used familiarities as their base. These clans lived nomadic lifestyles, which formed into hunting and food gathering societies. Clans studied grazing behaviors of large animals (of which they considered as a source of food) and followed them for thousands of miles, from one edge of a continent to another edge. Some clans even followed animals across straits of land from one continent to another.

Large clans were essential because it was common to loose members when hunting large prey, or during long and tedious treks, or during fatal clashes with other clans over hunting territories or over women. It was very rare but not totally unheard of for a single clan to reach numbers into the mid hundreds to low thousands.

By the Neolithic Age (New Stone Age) 10,000 BC-4,000 BC, clans had hit upon the value of fertile river valleys. Clans discovered that fertile river valleys offered good drinking water, good cooking water, and good bathing water; furthermore, they adopted sedentary lifestyles, domesticated plants and animals, and they also contrived the proficiency of agronomy. This adaptation of agronomy facilitated their shift from hunting and gathering food to producing food; thus, ending their nomadic lifestyle.

As more clans arrived in these respective fertile river valleys, space became limited, boundaries were crossed, and deadly feuds ensued. To circumvent such dreadful disasters, usually the first clans, to arrive in a fertile river valley, would establish institutions to control the attitudes, behaviors, interest, and values of those who would populate the areas within and near a fertile river valley. This social control was incorporated into institutions and formed enclaves called municipalities; hence, humans became city dwellers i.e., civilized.

The institutions that were formed included economics, education, family, politics, and religion. Clans assembled a concept of managing the consumption, distribution, and production of people's material needs. They gave these concepts principles, and called those principles economics. In the same token, clans collected all the knowledge they obtained from planting crops, observing animals, and humans, the weather, the sun, the moon, among other things. Then developed plans to train and teach this knowledge to others; as a result, this process was termed education. Moreover, clans homage the natural attraction between a man and woman, gave titles and roles to them and their relatives. This process established the family. Also clans embraced the customary practice of humans negotiating and compromising with each other. They gave this practice rules, and called this practice politics. Finally, clans espoused an old belief that a great arrangement of energy created the world and everything in it. This belief was straddled with rituals and dogma which brought into being religion.

As just stated, during the Neolithic Age, humans established the institution of family for social control. It was during this Age that the concept of a legal bond of marriage was conceived which was defined as, the state of being united to a person, of the opposite sex, as husband and wife. At the start of the new age, AD 2000, this definition of marriage has become the subject of discussion. In this 7th voice, let's note that the hearts of many Americans (including African Americans) are hardened against this traditional model of marriage.

Jesus Would Support Same Sex Marriages

On Wednesday, May 9, 2012, President Barack Obama became the first sitting United States President to announce his support for same sex marriage. For many of President Obama's faithful Christian followers his announcement became a dilemma. Some of his followers wanted to support him but their religious beliefs had them questioning the spiritual stability of the President.   This was only a dilemma because some Christians had linked their soul to a Mosaic law when they should have linked their soul to the teachings of Jesus. When Jesus lived (about 2,012 years ago) he did not speak out in favor of same sex marriage but in his teachings there is precedence to prove that if Jesus walked among us today he would cosign President Obama's decision to support same sex marriage.

It is said that six hundred years before Jesus was born a 33-year-old Chinese philosopher, named Confucius, believed the same way as many Christians today. China, during the late Chou Dynast (6th Century BC), was considered by many as Satan's summer and winter resort of the Far East. This chaotic culture was filled with destitution and ignominy of the highest degree. As in all ages of debauchery and lawlessness, this particular period was marked by the warring states of China.

It seemed every state in China had its own King and its own army. These Chieftains fought hard for the whole of China. This fighting included beheading prisoners of war and innocent women, children, and the aged. Those who were spared were forced to drink the human soup of those whose who were thrown into boiling caldrons. Since each and every state was in upheaval the aesthetic, moral, and philosophical aspects of humans were being over shadowed by oppressive political systems, exploitive economic systems, and degrading social systems that embraced a man's right to rape any woman at will.

As fate would have it, from this bottomless pit crawled Confucius, a learned but sincere statesman who happened to be disturbed by the lack of concern and respect that was made apparent in human relationships. He was also appalled by the way politicians justified their ends to a dishonest means that enabled them to achieve their goals.

Confucius went throughout China teaching only that the renewal of antiquity can rid China of its social problems. When the 86 year old Lao-tse heard Confucius' teachings he scolded Confucius by saying: "Ancient ceremonies and old-time forms cannot revive China. Obedience to the letter of the law must give way to the life of the spirit."

"The letter of the law must give way to the life of the spirit." What does that mean? It means the people of a particular age determines the relevance of laws. You always hear people say "you can tell what is going to happen by the sign of the times". Remember; when the times change, the laws must reflect that change.

During the days of Jesus, the people did not question him about same sex marriage because during Jesus's time the people still supported the Leviticus law (18:22) "Thou shalt not lie with mankind, as with womankind: it is

abomination". Instead, the people questioned Jesus about

the law that grants a man the right to put away his wife

(divorce). In that conversation Jesus establishes the

precedence for the same sex marriage argument of today,

AD 2012.

According to the 19th chapter of Matthew, religious

leaders went to Jesus to ask him about a man's right to put

away his wife (divorce) for any reason. Jesus explained

that there are elements to getting a divorce such as

fornication; but, he did not stop there. Jesus went on and

quoted the law: "What therefore God hath joined together

let not man put asunder (divorce)." According to Jesus,

during the time of Moses, the people's hearts where

hardened against that law so the letter of that law had to

give way to the life of the spirit. For this reason, Moses

concocted this concept called divorce; but according to Jesus, divorce was never in the Master's plan; therefore, it was a sin for a man to put away his wife.

Some believe that Abraham died about 246 years before Moses was born. The people, during the days of Abraham, did not question a man's right to put away his wife because the people still believed it was a sin and it was wrong. However, more than 200 years later the people were ready to change that law. Moses would roll over in his grave for the reasons people are getting a divorce these days. What are irreconcilable differences? That is not fornication. When we study Jesus' attitude on this subject of divorce it is clear he did not agree with the law, but he did acknowledge that it was what the people wanted. If Jesus were on scene today, I am convinced he would not agree with same sex marriage but if it is what two consenting adults wanted, he would not try to deny them of

it; after all, laws were made for man, man was not made

for laws.

8th Voice

According to Herodotus, the Ancient Greek historian, all the people from Ancient Ethiopia to India were Black; for this reason, African Americans identify with the legacy of Ancient Egypt but, neither history nor DNA supports the theory that African Americans are descendants of Ancient Egyptians. Another reason African Americans are fascinated with Ancient Egypt is because many western European nations (including United States of America) professes Ancient Egypt as the cradle of their civilizations. When African Americans were stripped of their West African cultures, they were forced to espouse the cultures of their oppressor. The USA and other European nations, has Ancient Egyptian motifs woven throughout its culture and for this reason many African Americans have adopted Ancient Egyptian symbols. African Americans origin is in West Africa and Ancient Egypt is not the cradle of West African cultures. Ancient Egypt is not the cradle of the Oyo Empire, the Akan Empire, the Dahomey Empire, the Benin Empire, the Bubi people, the Balanta people, nor the Tikar people. In the USA on the back of the one dollar bill, there is an Ancient Egyptian pyramid and the all Seeing Eye of Horace. What if instead of Ancient Egyptian symbols, on the back of the one dollar bill, it displayed an Ifa Divination Tray and the trident of Olokun? Would African Americans reconsider the intrinsic value West African symbols? African Americans were taught to revere Ancient Egypt and despise West African cultures. This eighth voice is dedicated to Imhotep, one of African American's favorite Egyptians.

MHTP: The Egyptian Polymath

Imhotep was a brilliant contriver whose contributions to the lifestyle of Ancient Egypt intensified the imaginations of the occultists, philosophers, and scientists of Greece and Rome; however, many of the attributes attributed to this great contriver are wrongfully ascribed. After one researches other individuals of the same name, it behooves that the historical figure that has survived the politics of history as Imhotep is but a composite character, composed out of the accomplishments, attributes, and greatness of other men named Imhotep.

Not much is known of Imhotep's early history; however, bits and pieces have been collected into the legacy of Imhotep, which begins with his father. Imhotep's father was an architect named Kanofer and his mother's name was Khreduonkh; Imhotep's wife's name was Ronpe-nofret.[2] Scholars have yet to obtain any substantial information that pertains to Imhotep's early years or information as to his training and education; nevertheless, he is regarded as Egypt's father of architecture, father of medicine, and father of sculpture. In addition, he is also credited with landscaping the world's first step pyramid in Sakkarah (Sokari) for the Pharaoh Zoser (Djoser) (2980-2900 BCE), the greatest Pharaoh of the Third Dynasty.[3]

Not only did Imhotep build Zoser's pyramid but he was also Zoser's vizier (overseer of works, mayor) with a

[2] Jamieson B. Hurry, Imhotep-The Egyptian god of Medicine (Chesapeake: ECA Associates, 1990) 24.

[3] Rudolph r. Windsor, From Babylon to Timbuktu (Atlanta: Windsor's Golden Series, 1988) 57.

jurisdiction as far reaching as the sun's rays. Along with these feats, Imhotep is hailed as the inventor of the art of construction in dressed stone; as well as the world's earliest physician, "chief judge; overseer of the king's records; bearer of the royal seal; chief of all works of the king; supervisor of that which Heaven brings, the Earth creates and the Nile brings. Supervisor of everything in this entire land"[4] and an astronomer.

The various careers of Imhotep have been cited only so the reader is somewhat familiar with all that he has been said to have accomplished. Before we discuss if one man did indeed do all the feats stated above, let us first examine the casual use of certain names in Ancient Egypt.

When the successions of rulers are from a single family's bloodline, that particular period of family reign is termed a Dynasty. Often Family rulers, of Ancient Egypt,

---

[4] Hurry, 6.

were named after ancestors who had ruled as Pharaohs and Queens. As a result, family members were usually identified as so and so I, II, III, et cetera. This was done for the purpose of correctly and honestly recording the deeds and accomplishments of the right family member; for example, Amenhotep II, Amenhotep III, and Thutmose I, Thutmose II.

One of such names was that of Cleopatra. The name Cleopatra was commonly passed down to heirs of the thrown in Ancient Egypt. Cleopatra VII lived (69-30 BCE) during the Thirtieth Dynasty.[5] It was an Egyptian custom to deify their Pharaohs and Queens. Not only was Cleopatra VII a Queen but also, she was beautiful. In line with her sensuous nature, she "was worshipped as the greatest of all goddesses, the Virgin Mother Isis."[6] This

---

[5] J.A. Rogers, <u>World's Great Men of Color: Vol. I</u> (New York: Macmillan Publishing company, 1972) 121.
[6] Rogers, 124

particular Cleopatra gained her fame by being brilliant, gorgeous, and insatiable; so much so, until she literally captivated the intangible combustion that resided in the bosoms of first, Julius Caesar and later, Mark Anthony.

By the age of seventeen, Cleopatra VII was well learned in the ways of Egypt and she was also well versed in several diverse languages. With the desire to see her people's ancient culture, dignity, and identity remain intact, Cleopatra VII used her charm, intellect, and wisdom to seduce two of the most powerful world leaders.[7] While under her spell of deep and tender feelings of affection the two men strove to fortify, protect, and uplift Egypt instead of subduing and conquering it, which was their original occupation.

---

[7] Rogers, 121-129.

After Julius Caesar was assassinated (the first of the Romans to become smitten by Cleopatra's strong and passionate affection), Mark Anthony became co-ruler of Rome (the other two rulers being Lepidus and Octavius). Anthony, during his military campaign in Egypt, fell madly in love with Cleopatra VII. This love drove him to renounce his allegiance to Rome and vowed to conquer Rome as a state of Egypt. Octavius defeated Anthony. This defeat drove Anthony to commit suicide.[8]

Although there were other Queens in Egypt of the same name, Cleopatra VII is the only one who's deeds and accomplishments have survived the test of time. Unlike Imhotep, history has not been as tempted to question the accomplishments accredited to Cleopatra VII; yet, there are those who have presumptions about her African or non-African heritage. The African strain of Cleopatra

---

[8] Rogers, 127.

VII's heritage had not been contested until the doctrine of "White race superiority". This doctrine was spearheaded by the German scholar, Johann F. Blumenback (1752-1840).[9]

The purpose of this doctrine was to dispel the notion that two of Europe's greatest white men became lovesick over a Black woman. It seems for this reason Cleopatra VII was made white and it would also explain why Hollywood would portray her as a white woman in the 1963 movie *Cleopatra*, which starred Elizabeth Taylor. As of Cleopatra VII, it has been said her mother was of Asiatic heritage and positioned herself into the Egyptian Royal circles, during the Persian invasion of the Twenty-seventh and Twenty-eighth Dynasties. In contrast, her father Ptolemy XIII, as the illegitimate child of the Pharaoh Ptolemy XI (Soter II).[10]

---

[9] Windsor, 21.
[10] Rogers, 130.

History as of late appears to be satisfied with the possibility of one woman possessing the beauty, brains, and sexuality needed to manage a government and seize and hold the focus of two of Rome's greatest leaders. Maybe if it was said that along with her accomplishments, just cited, she also produced incredible works, in volumes, on geography; waged and won a war against Octavius; and traveled to Mesoamerica and built the Olmec pyramids. Then it is likely that the fate of doubt would cause a detailed investigation into the lives of perhaps all the Cleopatras, for the purpose of determining which Cleopatra did what and exactly how did she do it? As of now, the deeds of Cleopatra VII are not being questioned because history is satisfied with the accounts accredited to her.

Another Queen of eminent distinction was Queen Nefertari, wife of Ahmose I, founders of the Eighteenth

Dynasty. Ahmose I and Nefertari ushered in a legacy of rulers whose likeness, in ruler ship and diplomacy had not been seen since the Fourth Dynasty.

It appears that after the Fourth Dynasty, domestic unrest caused the political foundation, of Ancient Egypt, to eventually break into pieces. This in turn made way for the Hyksos (Hebrews) from Palestine to settle in and live as Egyptians during the Eleventh and Twelfth Dynasties (1645-1567 BCE).[11]

For a Queen of Egypt to be named Nefertari was quite passé; nevertheless, anthropologist and historians are comfortable with naming Nefertari, of the Eighteenth Dynasty, as the greatest of the Queens with that name. This title is based on Nefertari's active participation in leadership, her diplomacy in the national affairs,[12] and the administrative development of her son, Amenhotep I.

---

[11] Chancellor Williams, <u>The Destruction of Black Civilization</u> (Chicago: Third World Press, 1976) 42.

Like Cleopatra VII, of the Thirtieth Dynasty, the recorded accomplishments attributed to Nefertari, of the Eighteenth Dynasty, appears to have been attainable by one woman in one lifetime. On the other hand, if it was recorded that among Nefertari's renowned accomplishments included a self-production of magnificent works, in volumes, on biology and physics, and that she also planted and nurtured the Hanging Gardens of Babylon, then maybe the lives of each Nefertari would be examined to determine which Nefertari accomplished what feat. As of now history appears to be pleased with the possibility of one woman accomplishing the things that are attributed to just one Nefertari. If not, I am sure scholars would be crawling the streets of Egypt looking for explorations to "Wonder Woman".

---

[12] Williams, 113.

Imhotep, of the Third Dynasty, is but one of the Great Imhoteps of Ancient Egypt. Unlike the common practices that occurred within Dynasties, where a person inherited the name of an ancestor, it appears that the Imhoteps of Ancient Egypt were not related. These non-related Imhoteps seem to be the case because although many great deeds were recorded under the name of Imhotep theses deeds werc achieved during different reigns; and while at least only one of the Imhoteps is recorded as being a Pharaoh, unlike other names, the name Imhotep was a popular name throughout the many Egyptian Dynasties. Who were those other Imhoteps and what did they accomplish? This will be discussed further on in this discourse. First, the reader must be aware that it is highly impossible for one man to have done all that is commonly associated with the accomplishments of Imhotep. To truly understand this critique on the legacy of

Imhotep one must be made aware of the critiques that gray headed scholars have heaped up on the legacy of Aristotle.

Aristotle was born in (384 BCE) at a town in Thrace called Stagira. It is said that Aristotle's father, Nicomachus, was the private physician to King Amyntas', ruler of Macedonia. At the age of seventeen, it is believed that Aristotle traveled to Athens to study at Plato's Academy for twenty years. When Plato died, (347 BCE), Aristotle moved to Assos, a city in Asia Minor, for a stint. Aristotle was thirty-seven years old. After King Amyntas' death Phillip, Amyntas' son, became ruler of Macedonia. Phillip offered Aristotle the position of tutoring Alexander, Phillip's son. After the assassination of Phillip, Alexander (B.K.A. Alexander the Great) became ruler of Macedonia.[13] As King Alexander (in 334 BCE) embarked upon an Egyptian and Asiatic campaign of concurring; in the

---

[13] Bertrand Russell, "A History of Western Philosophy", Simon & Schuster, 1972

meantime, Aristotle moved to Athens and founded a school called the Lyceum. After receiving a large sum of money, from Alexander, Aristotle purchased several volumes of books. After Alexander's death (in 323 BCE) the Athenian government began a campaign against Macedonian attitudes, interest, and values. For his pro-Macedonian behavior, a priest named Eurymedon indicted Aristotle for impiety by a priest named Eurymedon.[14] Aristotle then fled to a family estate, to a city, in Euboea, called Chalcis, where he died in 322 BCE

Aristotle's legacy classifies him as author of a thousand books on such subjects as Art, Economics, Ethics, Mathematics, Physics, Poetry, Politics, Rhetoric, and Theology. As of late, scholars have declared that the feats accredited to Aristotle were not capable of being done by him. This conclusion was drawn based on the fact

[14] George G. M. James, <u>Stolen Legacy</u> (San Francisco: Julian Richardson Associates, 1988) 113.

that for twenty years Aristotle studied under the direction of Plato. While Plato was famed as a philosopher, he was not qualified to train Aristotle as a scientist; furthermore, Plato's professor, Socrates, did not teach the subjects of Economics, Mathematics, or Politics.[15] So, how could Aristotle have learned these complex subjects from Plato?

Recently, scholars have declared that a portion of those twenty years that was originally believed that Aristotle spent under the tutelage of Plato was actually spent under the tutelage of an Egyptian Priest.[16] Scholars also believe that when Alexander stormed into Egypt (in 332 BCE) Aristotle rode in on Alexander's coat tail. After Aristotle secured the books in the Alexandrian Library, he copied the information from them and presented them as his own.

---

[15] James, 127.
[16] Jamess, 130.

Indeed modern scholarship has shown that the writings of Aristotle bare all the marks of hurriedly copied notes which of course suggest that Aristotle himself copied those notes from the books of the Alexandrian Library. The historical account of Aristotle's life is incredible".[17]

This recent in-depth investigation of Aristotle's claims were due to the fact that after Aristotle spent twenty years of studying, he was thirty-seven years old; moreover, he died twenty-five years later. As a result, scholars have determined that twenty-five years or even sixty-two years are not enough time for one man to produce a thousand books on such complex subjects.

In the same spirit of investigating the career of Aristotle, it is only scholastically correct that learned persons would analyze, examine, and question the actual possibility of Imhotep accomplishing the accolades

---

[17] Ibid.

attributed to him. To circumvent a person, such as Aristotle, from ever receiving acknowledgments that they falsely deserve, some scholars created a system of identifying when a mistake has been made in the area of awarding accomplishments of historical figures. One such scholar is George G. M. James. While concluding his systematic inquiry of Aristotle's career, James set a precedence that must also be considered in this search into the career of Imhotep.

> "How did Aristotle, a single individual, come to possess such a vast number of scientific works, a body of knowledge which took the Ancient World five thousand years or more to accumulate? It is evident that Aristotle's fame as a scholar has been grossly exaggerated: for such an accomplishment would have been both a physical and mental impossibility. Throughout the intellectual advancement of man, the world has witnessed many a genius; but those have always been specialists in particular fields, not specialists in every branch of science".[18]

Unlike the legacy of Aristotle, there are no recorded birth and death dates for Imhotep. Without these dates it is difficult to determine if Imhotep had the time to accomplish at least half of what is said he accomplished. There are also no dates as to when or if Imhotep studied in the Ancient Egyptian Mystery System or at the Grand Lodge of Wa'at. The most obvious question now is when, where, and how did Imhotep receive this large wealth of knowledge?

It is believed that the Egyptian priests were familiar with those sciences that explain the rudiments of the universe; however, the priests are known more for teaching secret lessons to Neophytes. Another thing that is interesting is nowhere else in Egyptian history is there a

---

[18] James, 129.

person who accomplished something that no one else has ever done.

Contrary to what many may know, there were several people, in Ancient Egypt, who lived under the name of Imhotep. When one examines Imhotep's life on the bias, it is practicable that he was an architect, a trade he may have learned from his father Kanofer, the great architect; therefore, when we apply James' theory into the life of Imhotep it seems possible that Imhotep could have designed Zoser's Step Pyramid at Sakkarah. Is it also possible that this Imhotep did great wonders as a vizier and physician, when there are no records to prove that he was ever trained in these trades? These dilemmas are problematic to the natural flow needed to record a history that will reflect an earnest portrait of human nature and human capabilities. This forces scholars to examine the lives of the other individuals of the name, Imhotep.

When one thoroughly researches the ancient days of Egypt, one will stumble across several diverse persons of the name, Imhotep. One of the Imhotep's, one is likely to meet will be wearing the title of "Royal Scribe" and he will be living in Thebes during the Eighteenth Dynasty in the reign of the Pharaoh Amenophis III, a man of peace (1410-1375 BCE).[19] It would be a logical assumption to presume that the poetry and philosophical writings that are associated with Zoser's Imhotep actually belong to Amenophis III's Imhotep. As of Zoser's Imhotep, there are no writings attributed to him; on the other hand, there are ancient "Instructions" that have been left behind by the sage, Ke'Gemni, scribe of the Pharaoh Huni, last Pharaoh of the Third Dynasty; and Ptah-hotep, vizier to the Pharaoh Assa, of the Fifth Dynasty.[20] Yet, there are no writings

---

[19] Hurry, 25.
[20] Ptah-Hotep and Ke'Gemni, <u>The Instructions of Ptah-Hotep and Ke'Gemni</u> (Waddington: William Preston, 1990) 1-51.

that bear the name of Zoser's, Imhotep. The only conclusion is, Zoser's, Imhotep was not a scribe. On the contrary, he was an architect, and that is all he was. Likewise, there are no architectural wonders attributed to Amenophis III's Imhotep. The reason being that Amenophis III's Imhotep was a scribe, and that is all he was. By labeling these different Imhoteps, according to their historical contributions to the human race, it helps establish a mortal connection with the ancient people as humans and not fictitious super beings of some far-off ancient storage. When each individual is correctly cited for their works, it allows history to enjoy the humanity of each person and not immortalize one individual at the expense of others.

The rebuilding legacy of the Eighteenth Dynasty should include a poetic legacy as well; furthermore, the poetic writings that are usually attributed to the Third

Dynasty, Imhotep should be lifted from the Third Dynasty and transported to the Imhotep of the Eighteenth dynasty. This transporting of poetic writings, from one era to another, would explain the regalvanized interest in Imhotep during the Eighteenth Dynasty. Imhotep's reemergence is not a case of a lost and found poet. The Imhotep of the Third Dynasty was an architect, not a poet. Rather, it was a case where a poet was born in the Eighteenth Dynasty under the name Imhotep. Unfortunately, the identity of Amenophis III's, Imhotep of the Eighteenth Dynasty was merged with the identity of Zoser's, Imhotep of the Third Dynasty.

Another Imhotep of ancient Egypt lived during the twelfth Dynasty, as a famous official under the reign of the Pharaoh Sesostris (Senusert) (2,000-1700 BCE).[21] The duties of the famous official were that of vizier. As vizier,

---

[21] Hurry, 25.

it can be said that all the governmental positions cited as part of the accomplishments of Zoser's Imhotep can now be forwarded to Sesostris' Imhotep. It is believed that Imhotep is responsible for the cliché, "Let us eat and drink, for to-morrow we shall die."[22] The poem that contains this cliché was part of the lesson Imhotep taught to the people of Egypt. As vizier Imhotep was Egypt's chief lecturer. In the poem Imhotep is reminding the people that life is meant to be lived, so, while they are on this earth, they should be concentrating on enjoying life and try to live life to its fullest. The oldest version of this poem was found in a tomb of the Theban Pharaoh Antuf (Intef);[23] consequently, Antuf lived during the Twelfth Dynasty. This one discovery makes it more than likely that the Imhotep, of the Twelfth Dynasty, inscribed these words of wisdom in the tomb of the Pharaoh Antuf, being that they

---

[22] Rogers, 38.
[23] Hurry, 17.

were both from the same Dynasty. To continue to attribute these words to the Imhotep, of the Third Dynasty, would be a grave misfortune in the name of historiography. It would be foolish of scholars to overlook a man, of wisdom, and not recognize him in his own time.

Imhotep, of the Twelfth Dynasty, was a great speaker and a great governor; in contrast, his talents did not include architecture or medicine. The time is now for scholars to accept that history has made a mistake in the documentation of the historical figure known as Imhotep. This mistake appears to be an honest one. To right this wrong would not mean anyone is stupid for believing in this age old falsehood; on the contrary, this mistake, that has existed for centuries, happened because several men of the same name were fused as one. First, it needs to be stressed, for the sake of future scholarship that the identities of the Imhoteps from the Third, Twelfth, and

Eighteenth Dynasties were melted together and molded into one historical figure. The danger in doing so needs to be understood by later scholars; hence, when such brilliant, great, and talented figures are meshed as one, we have seen that this meshing robbed the Twelfth Dynasty of its wise vizier and this meshing robbed the Eighteenth Dynasty of its Royal Poet.

Although the Imhotep of the Third Dynasty is credited as being the God of Medicine not even legend has provided modern records with any patients that Imhotep supposedly have cured. What is documented, is that the Egyptians:

> "diagnosed and treated more than 200 diseases, among them 15 diseases of the abdomen, 11 of the bladder, 10 of the rectum, 29 of the eyes, and 18 of the skin. They knew how to detect disease by the shape, color, or condition of the visible parts of the body, as the skin, hair, nails, and tongue. They treated spinal tuberculosis, gallstones, appendicitis,

gout, rheumatoid arthritis, mastoid diseases, and dental caries. They practiced surgery, knew of auscultation, and extracted medicine from plants."[24]

Another thing that is strange is Imhotep was worshipped as a demigod (by 525 BCE) and then as a full-fledged God of Medicine (550 ACE).[25] During this process of deifying Imhotep, his father Kanofer, was deleted and replaced with Ptah, the father of the Gods. His mother, Khreduonkh, was worshipped as the mother of the Gods while, at the same time, his wife Ronpe-nofret, was worshipped as the wife of the Gods.[26]

Greek mythology teaches the Greek name for Imhotep is Imouthes (Imuthes); furthermore, the Greeks had a God of Medicine name Asklepios (Aesculapius). Yet during the Hellenism period, for some reason, Imhotep

---

[24] Rogers, 39.
[25] Hurry, 29-73.
[26] Hurry, 24 & 25.

and Asklepios were merged into one. Here we see that Imhotep was not just merged with other humans, but Imhotep was merged with deities.

Here again we are forced to embrace the Egyptian accounts of their culture to discover that never was a non-Pharaoh made into a God. The question that arises now is how then did Imhotep become a god? This one question is not researched or talked about. This may allow many to stand strong behind their preposterous notion that the Imhotep of Third Dynasty was actually a Physician; yet those same persons cannot discuss any of his patients.

This brings us to the research of Adolf Erman. According to Erman at least one of the Pharaohs, in Ancient Egypt, was named Imhotep.[27] It was part of the Egyptian custom to deify the Pharaoh or Queen. Only royal blood could become a god. A Pharaoh named

---

[27] Adolf Erman, A Handbook of Egyptian Religion (London: Constable, 1907) 217.

Imhotep does explain how the name Imhotep became deified. It was stated earlier that Cleopatra VII was worshipped as the Virgin Mother Isis. One can only speculate that the reason she was worshipped as the Virgin Mother, Isis, may have something to do with Cleopatra VII's struggle to keep her country in one piece.

According to the myth Osiris was a god who became a Pharaoh for the purpose of teaching the barbaric Egyptians the blessings of civilization. Osiris taught the people to plant food and govern themselves. Osiris had an evil, jealous brother named Set. After devising a lengthy plot, Set mused his brother and chopped him into fourteen pieces. Isis, Osiris' wife, traveled throughout Egypt in search to for the missing pieces of her husband, for the purpose of keeping his body in one piece. One can only imagine that Cleopatra VII was worshipped as Isis because Isis struggled hard to keep what she loved in one piece.[28]

A Pharaoh named Imhotep, coupled with the knowledge that the ancient Egyptians deified their Pharaohs and Queens, helps to explain how the name Imhotep became a god. Yet, it is such a pity that history does not afford the Common Era with information as to what Dynasty he was a part of nor does it provide information on what he did as Pharaoh? One thing, we can be for certain about is, the people loved him.

Unfortunately, not much has survived in terms of historical records. As a matter of fact, there is not much information on the Imhotep's of the Twelfth or Eighteenth Dynasties. The only Imhotep, whose legacy furnishes modern historians with as much as a minuscule view of the historical figure is the Imhotep of the Third Dynasty. The history of the Imhotep of the Third Dynasty is not equipped with how or when he was educated nor does it

---

[28] John G. Jackson, <u>Introduction to African Civilizations</u> (Secaucus: The Citadel Press, 1970), 126-27.

offer information on his dates of birth and death; in contrast, this minute cast on the Imhotep of the Third Dynasty is more than what has survived of the Imhoteps of both the Twelfth and Eighteenth Dynasties put together. Nevertheless, for the sake of historical likelihood, that which is known must be analyzed and utilized to properly represent what has happened in the life or development of a people, country, or institutions.

With several great men with the name Imhotep, but with so few details of their lives, this could tempt a less then noble character into exaggerating, falsifying, and fusing the names until all the accomplishments of many become that of one. It appears that it was much easier to blend the men together and form one composite figure that would stand as the genius of the Ancient world, whose great deeds would not be surpassed even thousands of years later. Although noble as it may appear, this type of poor scholarship defaces the science of history, it spoils completely the idea of human capabilities. And, it blots brilliant, hardworking, and honest men out of the prominence of eternity.

To ensure that a mistake of this magnitude does not happen again, scholars must study all the possible reasons why and how this happened in the first place. The reason why could be many from poor record keeping or a result of what happens when your enemies outlive you. The best way to avoid a mistake, as a scholar, is to report what you find and admit that which you do not. If history had introduced the Imhoteps, in their own glory, we would have a much healthier view of the people and culture of Ancient Egypt; instead, we are at awe over their legend because we have been admiring a period that may be made up of composite figures of history.

History is equipped with information on the existence of others named Imhotep

that were not mentioned in the duration of this discourse.

9th Voice

Jazz music was invented in the late 1890s; yet, by the first decade of the 20th Century, middle class African Americans still did not openly admit to enjoying jazz music. During that time, middle class African Americans only favored gospel and classical music. During the roaring twenties, middle class White Americans were venturing into night clubs in New York City that featured jazz bands and in no time began praising jazz as a new sophisticated art form that was fast tempo, yet soothing. Once middle class White Americans endorsed jazz, as an authentic genre, middle class African Americans permitted themselves to openly enjoy the music. This ninth voice is not a review of jazz music. Instead, it is a glimpse into the complicated way in which African Americans have improvised their humiliation, transformed their anger, interpreted their pain, and responded to feelings of despair. This ninth voice is about how the residue, from America's original sin, became America's favorite song. This ninth voice is about how shameful head rags were fashioned into beautiful head pieces. This ninth voice is not about jazz music.

Why Young African Americans Abandoned Jazz

The genre of music, known today as jazz, was created out of a traditional understanding of purposeful African art. Traditional African art was in no way created for art sake. Instead, traditional African art was created for social purposes. Those early African Americans had a spiritual connection to their ancestry which enabled them to intuitively grasp the gist of a traditional usefulness for African art. African Americans have made progress in the areas of society and politics; as a result, their music transformed. Through constant struggle and agitation African Americans, as well as their music, gained a quantity of social and political power. To fully understand the 21st Century purpose of jazz for young African

Americas, we must first understand the purpose of African American music and also examine the evolution of African American music from the days of enslavement through the mid-twenty-first century.

There is an old proverb, which teaches us; we did not inherit this legacy from our ancestors; instead, we are borrowing it from our children. A legacy, like all things that are borrowed, must be given to the rightful owner. The legacy of African American music does not belong to generations past. In fact, the legacy of African American music belongs to the generation that is managing it, manipulating it, and molding it to fit within their reality, their disposition, and their attitude. To truly appreciate the historical legacy of African American music there are two concepts one must be able to identify with. The traditional purpose of African art (sculptures, dance, music, literature, etc.) was for social value. It was not an African tradition to create art for art sake. Genetic memory is another concept one must understand before truly appreciating the historical legacy of African American music.

Traditional African art "was" not created for art sake.[29] I use the word "was" because during the 1884 Berlin Conference, Africa was partitioned by well-organized and deliberate European nations with the intent of colonization. As a result of colonial coercion the land, people, and culture of Africa became oppressed by European political systems, exploited by European economic systems, and degraded by European social systems.[30] So African art that at one time was created only for a social purpose is now created for an economic purpose. The new purpose for African art is to be housed

---

[29] Duerden, Dennis. <u>African Art</u>. London: Hamlyn 1974, 7.
[30] Jackson, John G. <u>Introduction to Africa Civilizations</u>. Secaucus, NJ: Citadel Press, 1990, 310.

in European and American museums, hung on European and American walls, and photographed for European and American books. Music and dancing, at one time, was for the yearly traditional African ceremonies and celebrations. It now serves to entertain vacationing European and American tourists, entertain concert ticket holders, and sell compact discs. I hope it is clear that when I make mentions of African art, I am speaking of art dictated by African tradition, not art dictated by western capitalism.

It has been documented by historians and DNA scientists that the Africans who were brought, by European slave ships to the new world, to be enslaved, came mainly from West Africa between the regions of the Senegal River and the Congo River.[31] This fact must be stated because the ethnic group in the United States of America who

---

[31] Jackson, John G. <u>Introduction to Africa Civilizations</u>. Secaucus, NJ: Citadel Press, 1990, 310.

identifies itself as African or Black American is the descendant of those Africans from numerous traditional African cultures. Their link to those traditional African culturists is evident not only in skin tone, hair texture, and body type but in their uncanny manner of producing, sustaining, and manipulating culture. The ultimate purpose of this discourse is to prove that the genetic roots of African American culturists is linked to traditional African culturists. The best way to explain this connection is by a controversial phenomenon called genetic memory.

The concept of genetic memory implies that the most important behaviors that are essential to the survival of a people are innately coded in the deoxyribonucleic acid, DNA, (by the generation who initially learned the behavior) to assure the survival of future generations.[32] Usually, literature on the topic tends to explain, for

---

[32] Nirenberg, Marshall, "Genetic Memory," <u>JAMA</u> 206 no.9 (1968): 1973-1977.

example, how the love of books or the desire of a person to become a professor is passed on from one generation to the next. For this essay I am using the concept in a more collective manner, i.e., a collective genetic memory. I tend to explain not how one person inherited certain inclinations but instead the genetic inheritance of a whole people. I am choosing the concept of collective genetic memory as a way to explain certain phenomenon in regard to showing the link from those who engaged in traditional African culture to African Americans. I chose this concept because it is the best available to explain when traditional Africans were brought to the territory, that would become the United States of America, important elements of their culture were forbidden. Elements such as the rhythmic power of the drum and ways of dancing were banned for several generations (two and three hundred years).[33] When

---

[33] Quarles, Benjamin. <u>The Negro in the Making of America</u>. New York: Collier Books, 1969, 16.

the traditional African father and mother were separated from their children, for such a long period of time, the knowledge, understanding, and behavior of the traditional African should have been lost. Nevertheless, soon after the end of slavery, the newly freed African began to play and dance in the manner of the traditional African. How is this explained since there was no institution in place to teach the freed Africans their culture? Scholars, such as John Blassingame, may argue that the enslaved Africans did indeed establish a culture that was unique to their situation and rooted in many elements of traditional African culture. Blassingame's research does a great job of explaining how some language patterns, folk tales, music, dances, and spiritual beliefs survived the "peculiar institution"[34]. In spite of this, it does not explain how the traditional usefulness of African art has survived.

---

[34] Nirenberg, Marshall, "Genetic Memory," <u>JAMA</u> 206 no.9 (1968): 1973-1977.

As stated before, art in traditional Africa had a specific purpose. The purpose of art stayed relatively the same because the specifics of the traditional African's life stayed relatively the same. In traditional Africa, Africans did not have to meet the same challenges nor face the same tasks, as enslaved and freed African Americans. African Americans are challenged with opportunities of acquiring economic and social mobility and they are faced with the dutiful task of grasping power and responsibility of being American citizens. As a result of their hard work and endless strivings, African Americans have met the challenges and have achieved many of the tasks; therefore, the specifics of the lives of traditional Africans and African Americans are poles apart. With the specifics of the lives of African Americans changing, so to have their art changed to meet their relative need of purpose.

Slave life was brutal, dehumanizing, and humiliating. To survive this peculiar and traumatic experience, Africans created a new art designed to aid them in contending with their new reality called plantation life. Upon their arrival in the new world Africans were seasoned into the correct behaviors and attitudes of being enslaved. Part of their seasoning process included a direct, painful, and methodical stripping of their forms of dance, their language, and their religious practices. After being taken from their homeland and stripped of their whole way of life, Africans had no other choice but to study their new captors and figure out what tool they could use to sustain themselves until they would be free from their wretched condition. After learning the new language and new spiritual beliefs, of the plantation life, Africans were able to create a new art form through which they could express their longings and hopes; comfort themselves from their heavy burdens; and send coded messages to one another. During the days of slavery this new art form was known as plantation songs. Today they are called Negro spirituals. Along with the stripping of their language and spiritual beliefs, Africans were also forbidden to use the drum. The drum was essential in traditional African culture because it was used to not only provide the foundation for musical ensembles but for communication as well. Through a skilled and complicated process of phonetic reproduction, Africans were able to construct sophisticated channels of communication, which enabled them to send announcements over long distances.[35]

After studying their captive's religion (Christianity), Africans realized that it contained colorful stories of a promise made by a great and revengeful God that would

---

[35] Roberts, John. <u>Black Music of Two Worlds</u>. New York: Schirmer Books, 1998, 22.

vanquish the enemy of the enslaved, the despised, the rejected, the unloved, and the unwanted. The Africans saw those stories as symbolic of their situation. They saw hope in biblical stories about the anguish, liberation, and fortune of Jacob's son, Joseph; they saw hope in the suffering and deliverance from Egyptian bondage of the children of Israel; they saw hope in David's victory over Goliath; and they drew hope from the deliverance of Daniel from the lion's den and the deliverance of Daniel and the three Hebrew boys from the fiery furnace.[36] In traditional African culture, Africans worked long hours in the fields growing vegetables. In the fields they would sing work songs that helped pass the time. Since their work songs had been stripped from them during their seasoning process, the Africans had no other choice but to create a new art (plantation songs) from inspirational themes they

---

[36] Blassingame, John. The Slave Community. New York: Oxford University Press, 1972, 19.

found in their new religion. The new songs were sung in the fields, in spiritual or religious ceremonies, and they were used to send coded messages. Coded messages were about uprisings or escape attempts. The most prominent coded messages were those that announced the next escape by way of the Underground Railroad. Harriet Tubman was one of the most renowned conductors on the Underground Railroad. Tubman was often referred to as Moses. Moses was a heroic figure of the new plantation religion because she was renowned for safely leading enslaved Africans to freedom. Tubman was actually one of the conductors of the Underground RailRoad, which was a clandestine route of travel that consisted of secret trails and stations. A station was a brief lodging for rest and food in private homes that all led to the "promised land". That is, territories where Africans could live as free men and women either in the United States of America or Canada.

When songs such as "Go Down Moses" or "Swing Low Sweet Chariot" were sung it was a call to all those who were interested in "stealing away" for freedom and to be ready because Moses would be conducting her secret mission soon.[37] To their European enslavers and overseers those were just simple songs of faith.[38]

For the enslaved Africans, the purpose of plantation songs was to deaden the brutal blow of slavery, to galvanize their spirit from the dehumanization of slavery, and to dignify themselves as a result of the humiliating nature of slavery. Africans of the late 1860's to mid-1870's began life as freed (second class) citizens of the United States of America. This citizenship was both a blessing and a curse. It was a blessing being that these were the first Africans born after emancipation. Instead,

---

[37] Jones, Leroi. Blues People. New York: Morrow Quill Paperbacks, 1968, 26.
[38] Africana: The Encyclopedia of the African and African American Experience, 1999 ed. "Gospel Music," Richard Newman, 1777.

they were born into a world of hope. They had opportunities of having a career, acquiring an education, owning property, or migrating to the north to pursue life, liberty, and happiness. On the other hand, their freedom was a millstone because the U.S. government did little and more often nothing to curtail the vicious violence that stemmed from white America's racial hatred that fueled for slavery. This new generation of freed Africans began their life during the Reconstruction Era (1866-1877). It was during that era that men who were once enslaved became statesmen. These men introduced and helped pass many laws that created facilities in the south that did not exist before slavery began. The most noted laws that came from this era of these newly freed African legislators were in the areas of education, women suffrage, city government reform, and the jury system.[39] Although the

[39] Bradford, Sarah. Harriet Tubman: The Moses of Her People. Bedford, Massachusetts: Applewood Books, 1993.

newly freed Africans proved they could make improvements in the south, their former enslavers still refused to share the responsibility of governing the south with their former slaves. Instead, southern whites under the shield of the 1876 Hayes Compromise were successful at ending the Reconstruction era by removing federal soldiers (in place to protect the rights of the newly freed Africans) and swiftly ushered in a new era of white supremacy called the Jim Crow Era (1877-1964).[40] Thousands of Blacks migrated north in fear of callousness that would emerge as a result of the soldiers leaving.

During the Jim Crow Era Black men in the south were legally stripped of many of the rights they gained during Reconstruction, including their right to vote. Southern whites intended to re-season the freed Africans

---

[40] Africana: The Encyclopedia of the African and African American Experience, 1999 ed. "Gospel Music," Richard Newman, 1775-1778.

by using violence and fear to force them into a submissive role in the south. The fear of vigilante mobs and hate organizations, such as the Ku Klux Klan, maimed and killed blacks and sympathetic whites who continued to fight for human and civil rights on behalf of southern blacks.[41] Southern Blacks were illegally slaughtered by mob violence. The violence included castrating, quartering, hangings, and many were burned alive. When these illegal vigilante mobs attacked defenseless freed Africans southern courts and legal systems failed to protect them. Therefore, they became overcome by feelings of helplessness and fear because the culprits were never accused of a crime, let alone indicted.[42] The victims were usually accused of minor incidents and were lynched without having a day in court. Their offenses were trivial

---

[41] Franklin, John Hope. From Slavery to Freedom. New York: Alfred A. Knopf, 1974, 257-259.

[42] Franklin, John Hope. From Slavery to Freedom. New York: Alfred A. Knopf, 1974, 264-267.

and petty, like disagreeing with a white man, refusing to give up farmland, accusations of raping a White woman, accusations of murdering a White person, unpopularity, and mistaken identity.[43]

During the days of bondage, the enslaved Africans longed to breathe free and they were able to express themselves through the advent of plantation songs. Incidentally, the Africans born during the Reconstruction Age did not have the same longings, because they were born free. Therefore, plantation songs did not have the same social meaning as they did during the days of slavery. As a reaction to their genetic memory, this new African born after slavery developed out of necessity two new genres of music that would relate to a soul that was freed yet caged (Blues and Ragtime). Blues music would

---

[43] Rogers, J.A. The Ku Klux Spirit. Baltimore, Maryland: Black Classic Press, 1980.

respond to the depressive feeling of seeing freedom but not able to touch it; of smelling freedom but not able to taste it; of saying "I'm free" but not able to take pleasure in it; that is the source of Blues music[44]. The music, lyrics, and delivery of those early Blues songs expressed the painful reality of Jim Crow. For many, anyone on hard times is considered as having the blues. This could not be further from the truth because during the Jim Crow Era, any southern White man who was on hard times i.e., poor, uneducated, with a large family, and out of work could take his violent and deadly frustrations out on any southern Black man, woman, or child. This is "what the blues was all about". Because Blues was generated from within the pain of Jim Crow, it continued to have a social significance until well within the next era of Civil Rights.

---

[44] Jones, Leroi. <u>Blues People</u>. New York: Morrow Quill Paperbacks, 1968, 26.

The other genre of music responded to the portion of the soul that had expressed a gleeful feeling of being free. Although the Jim Crow era was gloomy, the new African still had hope because he could grow crops for his family, get an education and become a leader in his community, or ride on the above ground railroad to northern cities. This new feeling of hope was refreshing to the African whose soul was bitter from inherited feelings of the dreads of slavery. Although the new African knew he was caged, he still had a song in his heart. He expressed his new song through a musical genre called Ragtime.[45]

The gleeful spirit of Ragtime only represented the hopes of economic and social mobility of the new African American. By the early 1900s (1900-1920), African Americans had begun to taste the fruits of freedom. By the

---

[45] Africana: The Encyclopedia of the African and African American Experience, 1999 ed. "Ragtime," Eric Bennett, 1585.

1920s, African Americans were graduating from colleges and universities; they were becoming entrepreneurs; they were establishing sophisticated Greek letter organizations; membership in secret societies were increasing; and they were adopting the attitudes, interests, and values of middle class White America.

As a reaction to their genetic memory, these new haughty Africans moved toward originating two more new genres of music that would prove relevant to their newfound social identity. One genre was Jazz music and the other genre was gospel music.

Ragtime was created by Africans that expressed hopes of economic and social mobility in America. As a result of the African's creativity, unity, bravery, and hard work, a Black middle class was established. By the 1920s, more than one million Black people had migrated from the south to the north, and a measure of this economic and social mobility had been reached. One of the most celebrated people of that era was Madam C.J. Walker. Walker had amassed a fortune by offering a service to Black women only[46]. In addition, by the 1920s, Black people had made accomplishments, in various fields of endeavor. It prompted Dr. Carter G. Woodson to establish, in 1915, the Association for the Study of Negro Life and History (now the Association for the Study of Afro-American Life and History). In 1916, he founded the Journal of Negro History (now the Journal of African American History). And in 1926, he launched Negro History Week (now Black history month). Woodson went to these great lengths so Black accomplishments in such areas as science, business, and education could be well documented and acknowledged. Once again, musicians

---

[46] Bundles, A'Lelia Perry. <u>On Her Own Ground</u>. New York: Scribner, 2001..

were on the pulse of Black people and responded to these great accomplishments by creating music that was based on improvisation; which was the best way to express the spirit of this new African's intellect. In just the second generation of freed Africans their condition had seemingly made a spontaneous metamorphosis. The music of this era signified racial pride, promise, and gleefulness. This new gleeful way of life gave way to jazz music, which was the fulfillment of ragtime[47].

The other genre of music to flourish during this time was gospel music. Gospel music was the first form of African American music to originate outside of the south.[48] During the days of slavery, Africans were not allowed to worship in their traditional African fervor which included group participation, shouting, and a spirit induced

---

[47] Africana: The Encyclopedia of the African and African American Experience, 1999 ed. "Ragtime," Eric Bennett, 1585.
[48] Africana: The Encyclopedia of the African and African American Experience, 1999 ed. "Gospel Music," James Clyde Sellman, 850.

spontaneity. When Blacks migrated to the north, they were in search of a whole new way of life. They wanted a life of passion, spontaneity, emotion, and above all, freedom. Along with everything else, this new northern life gave way to a new religious expression. Not only did the preaching meet the expectations of these new northern Black congregations, but the music changed too. In the late 1800s, White evangelicals created revival music that they called gospel songs. The lyrics of this revival music were appealing to these newly migrated Black people, because gospel songs spoke to their situation, their wants, and their desires. Whereas, plantation songs were coded and they expressed Black people as a collective "we". When Black people migrated to the north they wanted to redefine a life for themselves as individuals.[49] The revival songs were perfect because they spoke of Jesus delivering

---

[49] <u>Africana: The Encyclopedia of the African and African American Experience</u>, 1999 ed. "Gospel Music," James Clyde Sellman, 851.

the individual, personal salvation, and the language was emotional. These themes are evident in the early gospel songs such as, Thomas Dorsey's <u>Take My Hand, Precious Lord;</u> Lucie E. Campbell's <u>In the Upper Room With My Lord;</u> and William Herbert Brewster's <u>Move On Up a Little Higher.</u> It should be reiterated that gospel music did not spring from the souls of Black folk; however, Black folk did adopt it, baptize it, and made it their own. Although, today, African Americans are several generations past the origin of gospel music, the purpose of it still remains. Incidentally, gospel music allows African Americans to worship their god with freedom, passion, spontaneity, and emotion.[50]

As an example, to the profound extent of racial pride, promise and gleefulness, this same era of African

---

[50] <u>Africana: The Encyclopedia of the African and African American Experience,</u> 1999 ed. "Gospel Quartets," Eric Bennett, 856.

Americans are also responsible for the Swing Bands of the 1920s and 1930s: Bee-Bop, Boogie-Woogie, and Rhythm & Blues. The music in Black America was changing quick as never before because the deep syncopated winds of change were thrashing against America's social walls and the strong heavy back beat of time was proving to be the demise of Jim Crow.

African Americans born during and right after America's Great Depression was the generation that changed America forever. As always, the musicians were in tune with the pulse of the people. As did earlier generations, this new generation would express racial pride, promise, and gleefulness; unlike the others, this new generation would also express anger. As a result of education and living in neighborhoods with numerous Black doctors, lawyers, businessmen, and other professionals, this generation had come to the conclusion that not only were Black people just as intelligent and capable as Whites, but were also as deserving of the same equal treatment under the law as Whites. In view of this new awareness, this "new Negro" was angry about the legacy of slavery. They were intolerant to the open hostilities of Jim Crow. They wanted an end to racial discrimination in the north. They wanted an end to lynchings in the south. And as did the previous generations, they wanted economic and social mobility. In addition, this time they also wanted civil and human rights. This new attitude would be the driving force behind two new genres of music that would emerge from a very emotive Black community (Soul and Funk).

The possibility of racial equality became palpable in the late 1940's when President Harry Truman emitted his

Fair Deal policies. Fair Deal policies required the federal government to integrate the armed services, to practice fair employment in other federal services, and to implement public proclamations, supporting the improvement of conditions for African Americans.[51] Other industries, such as, aircraft, automotive, chemical and electronics increased the employment of African Americans as well. The government's initiative and also the advancements in men's professional sports meant that all at once White superiority had no social legitimacy.[52] Now, the battle would be to eliminate its legal power. By the mid 1950's, African Americans had mounted a well-organized assault on America's Jim Crow laws. America's entire racial beliefs which included an updated orientation of Black people's place in America. African Americans peacefully

---

[51] Franklin, John Hope. From Slavery to Freedom. New York: Alfred A. Knopf, 1974, 463-465.
[52] Robinson, Eddie. Never Before, Never Again. New York: St. Martin's Press, 1999.

and fluently demanded the removal of any and all racial restrictions that interfered with them exercising their rights as American citizens. They wanted access to public facilities such as hotels, restaurants and schools. They demanded their right to live in neighborhoods they could afford but were denied because they were black. They also wanted federal protection under the law from individuals. And local and state governments that would seek to violate their human and civil rights; in essence, African Americans wanted to be totally integrated into the American society. This new era in American history is known as the African American Civil Rights era (1955-1966). Once again, the music in Black America (jazz, swing, bee-bop, boogie-woogie, and rhythm & blues) did not have the same social meaning as it once did. As a reaction to their genetic memory, this "new militant Negro", as did African Americans before them, moved toward originating a new genre of music that would act as theme music for this new radical African American, soul music.[53]

During the Civil Rights era, African Americans were as nonviolent and humble as slaves; yet, they were forceful, persistent, and uncompromising as monarchs. Nevertheless, this articulate, heady, and innovative generation of Africans peeved southern whites that refused to accept Black people as anything other than inferior. By 1966, Whites in Chicago demonstrated animatedly against integration; thus, reinforcing the notion that white superiority was a nationwide belief. This White obdurateness caused many Blacks (north and south) to become frustrated and pessimistic; therefore, triggering them to view integrating with Whites as insane. This, in

---

[53] Africana: The Encyclopedia of the African and African American Experience, 1999 ed. "Soul Music," James Clyde Sellman, 1755.

turn, compelled many Black people to revolutionize their world view as African Americans. Consequently, this new radical thinking (of 1966) marked the beginning of the Black Power Movement. During the Black Power Movement many African Americans changed their focus of struggle to four areas of concern:

1. Black people began striving for racial dignity and self-reliance, which they believed was only obtainable through economic and political independence.

2. Black people focused on improving and controlling their own communities instead of striving to integrate into white communities.

3. Black people accentuated the cultural heritage of African people on the continent and in the diaspora.

4. Black people rejected racism and imperialism throughout the world and united with people of color against their European oppressors.[54]

The Black Power Movement was revolutionary and the musical genre, called funk, accented the Black Power Movement and it was just as revolutionary; for example, funk lyrics were focused on Black pride and anger. The best examples of these are apparent in the earliest songs of that era, such as: James Browns' <u>Say It Loud (I'm Black and I'm Proud)</u>; Sly and the Family Stone's <u>Don't Call Me Nigger, Whitey</u>; and Parliament's <u>Chocolate City</u>.[55]

Those African Americans born during the Black Power Movement (late 1960's-mid 1970's) are the vanguard to the legacy of African American music at the turn of the 21st century. As a reaction to their genetic memory, these

---

[54] Ture, Kwame. <u>Black Power</u>. New York: Vintage Books, 1992, 34-56.
[55] <u>Africana: The Encyclopedia of the African and African American Experience</u>, 1999 ed. "Funk Music," James Clyde Sellman, 795.

African Americans moved toward originating a new genre of music that would prove relevant to their newfound social identity. As did generations past, this generation inherited both the aspirations and the unfinished struggles of the previous generation. The aspirations and benefits that were put in place by the previous generations succeeded in gaining fair housing. It eliminated open hostilities. It eliminated lynching. And it eliminated Jim Crow laws and signs that restricted Blacks from public and private facilities and institutions. On the other hand, the new generation inherited the unresolved anger of slavery and Jim Crow, institutionalized racism, police brutality, racial profiling, poorly funded public school systems, limited options and opportunities for true economic and political advancement, and a rejection of African American identity and culture. This generation of African Americans had drawn the conclusion that the concerns of middle-class White America did not coincide with the attitudes, interest, and values of this new generation. For that reason, many of this generation speculated that the avenues of success that were trekked by many White Americans were not readily available to Blacks. As more Whites became vocal in their stance against set asides and affirmative action it led this new generation of African Americans to establish a new culture (hip hop) as well as a new musical genre, rap. Instead of focusing on traditional White American ideas of success, this new generation settled on exonerating four elements that would assure the success of their generation. They chose to exonerate:

1. Cultural Pride

2. Racial solidarity

3. Collective survival of the race

4. Economic self-sufficiency

Hip Hop culture gave this generation of African Americans everything that White America's popular culture refused or could not. Hip Hop culture was "on point" because it was flexible; open to creativity; tolerant; supportive; protective; and most of all forgiving. Hip Hop culture was successful because it existed under the premise of "maybe if". Maybe if African people had not been enslaved; maybe if African people were not brutalized and lynched over so many years; maybe if African people were given a fair chance like Europeans and offered good jobs based on skills and education and not race and color; maybe if African people were not hated so and castigated all the time; then maybe African people would feel a part of the American society. Those in the hip hop community understood that African American households do not always have the economic support or the fatherly influence that one may need to have a stable home. Consequently, sometimes young African Americans have to face the world without the proper guidance and nourishing which often land them on the wrong side of the law and on the wrong side of an ethical decision. Maybe if African Americans were raised in households that fostered model futures of stability instead of fostering model futures of hustling, then the pace of African American life would not be as fast and the price of African American life would not be cut-rate. Those within the hip hop community were not as quick to judge and they showed compassion towards each other because they understood the pain and history of one another.[56]

With mainstream White America as the other America those in Hip Hop decided to create their own mainstream. For example, their own form of art (graffiti), their own form of dance (break-dance), their own styles of

---

[56] Ogg, Alex. <u>The Hip Hop Years</u>. New York: Fromm International, 2001.

clothing (their own clothing line), their own music (deejaying & Rapping), and their own form of expression. One example of expression is seen in their body art and hairstyles. In the past, middle class, white America viewed body art as rebel behavior, yet, there are professional basketball players validating this art form; furthermore, African Americans are also sporting variations of African braids or Dreadlocks as accepted hairstyles when in past years it was taboo. Rap music represents the bitter edginess that comes from a people existing in a hostile society who has been persecuted over a long period of time.

Since the days of enslavement, African Americans have responded to their genetic memory and created a music that complemented their social reality in America. The African tradition of producing art only for social value explains why the interests in so many genres of African American music have petered out.   Although genres such as blues and jazz no longer have the same social value, they still have economic value; for that reason, these art forms have survived in American society. This is accurate because America's capitalistic society has a way of marketing anything that feels, looks, sounds, and taste good. By the new millennium, these genres are studied in colleges and universities and appreciated by black and white middle class; thus, signifying distinction for those who are "cultured".

Those African Americans born between 1995 and 2005 created a new genre of music determined by how that generation felt about being in America. Bear in mind that generations before them have created a very different America. They have created an America which demands that certain long-standing companies (in major cities)

reveal their business transactions during slavery;[57]

affirmative action prevailed; and many old murders by Ku

Klux Klan members that at one time seemed unsolvable,

produced indictments, trials, and convictions; Barack

Obama elected, America's first African American

president and Kamala Harris, America's first female vice

president; and the highest-ranking female elected official

in U.S. history. Harris is also the first Asian-American and

the first African-American vice president. And this

generation will enjoy a sense of privilege and entitlement

that in past generations were relegated for white only.

Therefore, it is acceptable for one to believe that in a

matter of time the government of America will issue an

official apology for slavery and the illegal business and

violent actions during Jim Crow. Owing to the

---

[57] Kong, Deborah, "More cities want companies who do business with them to disclose past ties to slavery" Associated Press, June 19, 2003.

advancements, just mentioned, one must believe that some form of reparations for slavery and Jim Crow would be foreseeable. If that were the case, then it is plausible to believe that the unemployment rate for African Americans would decrease significantly police brutality should discontinue. And feelings of being an outsider would subside. If these things were to come to past, it is possible to finally see African Americans enjoying stability as citizens of America; hence, concluding the African American tradition of establishing a new genre of music every generation. In Africa, the society was stable and during the days of slavery life was repressively stable. In both instances, the music stayed the same as generations passed. It was only when African Americans were freed to improve their lot in America did their future in America become unpredictable. As a result, the music has been changing to denote the struggles of African Americans.

Therefore, it is sensible to anticipate a new genre of African American music around 2030. The only question that remains is, will that genre be from a stable African American generation or will it be the forerunner to stability of African American music that will arrive in the late 2060s?

Bibliography

Website: https://ifstudies.org/blog/the-majority-of-us-children-still-live-in-two-parent-families

Africana: The Encyclopedia of the African and African American Experience, 1999 ed.

Blassingame, John. The Slave Community. Oxford University Press, 1972.

Bradford, Sarah. Harriet Tubman: The Moses of Her People. Applewood Books, 1993.

Bundles, A'Lelia Perry. On Her Own Ground. Scribner, 2001.

Charters, Samuel. The Legacy of the Blues. Da Capo Press, 1977.

Duerden, Dennis. African Art. Hamlyn, 1974.

Erman, Adolf. A Handbook of Egyptian Religion. Constable, 1907.

Franklin, John Hope. From Slavery to Freedom. Alfred A. Knopf, 1974.

Ginzburg, Ralph. 100 Years of Lynchings. Black Classic Press, 1988.

Hurry, Jamieson B. Imhotep-The Egyptian God of Medicine. ECA Associates, 1990.

Jackson, John G. Introduction to Africa Civilizations. Citadel Press, 1990.

James, George G. M. Stolen Legacy. Julian Richardson Associates, 1988.

Jones, Leroi. Blues People. Morrow Quill Paperbacks, 1968.

Kong, Deborah, "More cities want companies who do business with them to disclose past ties to slavery" Associated Press, June 19, 2003.

Nirenberg, Marshall. Genetic Memory. JAMA 206 no.9 1968.

Ogg, Alex. The Hip Hop Years. Fromm International, 2001.

Ptah-Hotep and Ke'Gemni. The Instructions of Ptah-Hotep and Ke'Gemni. William Preston, 1990.

Quarles, Benjamin. The Negro in the Making of America. Collier Books, 1969.

Roberts, John. Black Music of Two Worlds. Schirmer Books, 1998.

Robinson, Eddie. Never Before, Never Again. St. Martin's Press, 1999.

Rogers, J. A. World's Great Men of Color: Vol. I. Macmillan Publishing Company, 1972.

Russell, Bertrand. A History of Western Philosophy. Simon & Schuster, 1972.

Tirro, Frank. Jazz: A History. Norton, 1977.

Ture, Kwame. Black Power. Vintage Books, 1992.

Williams, Chancellor. The Destruction of Black Civilization. Third World Press, 1976.

Windsor, Rudolph R. From Babylon to Timbuktu. Windsor's Golden Series, 1988.